Monograph Book

PREVALENCE AND DETECTION OF METHICILLIN RESISTANT
Staphylococcus aureus (MRSA)

Editor

Smriti Rekha Gogoi
Department of Microbiology, School of Life Science, Sikkim University, Tadong Gangtok, Sikkim, India.

Ashish Kumar Singh
Department of Microbiology, School of Life Science, Sikkim University, Tadong Gangtok, Sikkim, India.

Dr. Hare Krishna Tiwari
Department of Microbiology, School of Life Science, Sikkim University, Tadong Gangtok, Sikkim, India.

Published by

JPS Scientific Publications
India

Published by

JPS Scientific Publications, Tamil Nadu, India.
E.mail: jpsscientificpublications@gmail.com
Website: www.jpsscientificpublications@gmail.com

Published in India.

International Standard Book Number (ISBN): 978-81-940316-4-2

Contents

Chapter Number	Chapter Title	Page Number
1	Introduction	1
2	General Description and Identification of *S. aureus*	4
3	MRSA Infection and Antibiotic Resistance	7
4	Types of MRSA	10
5	Mechanism of Methicillin Resistance in MRSA	11
6	Prevalence of MRSA	15
7	Phenotypic Methods for detection of MRSA	23
8	Genotypic Methods for Detection of MRSA	26
9	Strategies for Treatment of MRSA	29
10	Conclusion	32
11	Future Prospective	34
12	References	35

Abstract

Methicillin-resistant *Staphylococcus aureus* (MRSA) are commonly associated with nosocomial infections and are usually resistant to many antibiotics. This review summarizes the current scenario of the prevalence of methicillin-resistant *Staphylococcus aureus* (MRSA) and their antibiogram pattern in national and international hospitals. The *mec*A gene which was acquired by horizontal gene transfer of the *Staphylococcal* gene cassette (SCC*mec*), responsible for the increase in methicillin resistance worldwide. This gene encodes an alternative penicillin-binding protein, PBP 2a which is responsible for methicillin resistance in MRSA. In the present study, MRSA prevalence increases drastically from hospital to hospital. The antibiogram of these isolates indicated widespread resistance to various groups of antibiotics *i.e.* penicillin, cephalosporins, carbapenems, vancomycin, tetracycline, chloramphenicol, streptomycin etc. Antibiotic sensitivity was performed by Kirby-Bauer disk diffusion method and minimum inhibitory concentrations were determined for vancomycin and methicillin according to CLSI guidelines. Different molecular methods like multilocus-sequence-typing (MLST), pulse-field-gel electrophoresis (PFGE), SCC *mec* typing were also used for detection of methicillin resistance in *S. aureus*. Thus this review comprehensively covers the epidemiology, clinical manifestation, and management of these clinical entities.

Key words: Methicillin-resistant *Staphylococcus aureus*, Prevalence, Antibiotics, *mec* genes

1

INTRODUCTION

Staphylococcus aureus often referred to as "staph" is a commonly occurring bacterium which normally resides on the skin or in the nose of a healthy person (1). *S. aureus* may cause certain skin infections, soft tissue infections such as boils and also causes severe infections such as wound infections, pneumonia, sepsis and abscesses (2). It is now identified as the drug-resistant pathogen worldwide. After the first use of penicillin in 1941, the penicillinase-producing *S. aureus* was identified in the year 1944 and was reported to show resistant to penicillin (3). *S. aureus* continues to be a harmful pathogen for both the hospital-associated as well as community-acquired infections. A report from the year 2010, shows that the community-acquired *S. aureus* infections are increasing at a higher rate (4) (5).

A report in the year 1961 showed that methicillin-resistant *Staphylococcus aureus* (MRSA) has become a major nosocomial pathogen worldwide (6). Methicillin-resistant *Staphylococcus aureus* (MRSA) has become resistant to most of the β-lactam antibiotics include penicillin, amoxicillin, methicillin, ampicillin, oxacillin, cephalosporins, carbapenems, chloramphenicol, tetracycline *etc* (7). The infection of MRSA may spread through direct contact with skin or through contaminated equipment (8).

The *mec*A gene is a part of *Staphylococcal* chromosome cassette *mec* (SCC*mec*) which is responsible for the resistance to methicillin which codes for the penicillin-binding protein (PBP2a),76KDa protein (9). The *mec*A gene transcription is repressed by the regulatory gene *mec*I and *mec*R1 (10). The *mec*I gene encodes a transcriptional regulator and the *mec*R1 gene encodes the membrane-bound signal transduction proteins. The PBP2a protein synthesis is regulated by the *mec*I and *mec*R1genes in the *bla*Z system (11). It was reported that when methicillin-resistant *S. aureus* was performed the MIC susceptibility test with oxacillin, *mec*A positive strain showed phenotypically susceptible to β-lactam antibiotics (12). It was experimentally found that when the methicillin is used by the patients the Penicillin-binding protein is inactivated and the PBP2a protein is expressed and the synthesis of peptidoglycan is induced (13).

The prevalence of MRSA has varied drastically from hospital to hospital in various countries. The Pennsylvania State College of Medicine, Hershey, Pennsylvania, USA reported that about 20% of the *S. aureus* isolates were methicillin-resistant in

Prevalence and Detection of Methicillin Resistant *Staphylococcus aureus* (MRSA)

Europe, whereas 33% to 55% of the prevalence rate of MRSA in US hospitals (14). A study period of 36 months from the year 2003-2005 was carried out from the southern to eastern Mediterranean countries, where 38% of the isolates were found to be resistant to MRSA. The highest proportion of MRSA was reported by Jordan, Egypt, and Cyprus where more than 50% isolates were methicillin-resistant (15). In a major tertiary surgical hospital, Benghazi, Libya, the study was conducted in April to July 2000, total 200 isolates were examined out of which 62 were methicillin resistant (16). The study was conducted in Nepal on the different clinical samples in which 112 *S. aureus* isolates out of 162 showed resistant to methicillin. This report showed a high prevalence of MRSA in Nepal (17).

The prevalence rate of MRSA in All India Institute of Medical Sciences (AIIMS) was 44% from December 2001 to March 2002 (18). The cross-sectional study of tertiary care hospital in Sikkim, India reported that about 152 isolates from 827 *S. aureus* isolates were resistant to methicillin (19). In Guru Tegh Bahadur Hospital, Delhi, a total of 319 samples was collected from nasal swabs, out of which 94 samples were found to be resistant to oxacillin (20). In India, several studies were conducted in a different hospital to study the antibiotic resistance among hospital-acquired *S. aureus.*

During the study period between 1 June 2002 to 31 August 2002, the prevalence rate was 3.0% out of 3.4% acquiring MRSA colonization. This study shows that the patients colonized with the MRSA were at higher risk (21). The MRSA can be detected by both phenotypic methods as well as genotypic methods. The detection of *mec*A gene of methicillin-resistant isolates can be difficult because the *mec*A gene differs in the level of expression of resistance (22). The phenotypic methods for detection of MRSA include the Oxacillin disk diffusion test, the oxacillin screen agar test, the cefoxitin disc diffusion test, minimum inhibitory concentration (MIC) *etc* (23). One of the studies reveals that the disc diffusion method for the detection of MRSA is a good alternative method for identification of intermediate resistant strains of *S. aureus* (24).

Different methods are implicated in the genotypic methods for detection of MRSA following the determination of *mec*A gene by PCR method (24) (25). Detection of the *mec*A gene using the minigel and color based PCR, detection of PBP2a using a commercial latex agglutination kit and detection of resistance to mupirocin by using Qiagen kit DNeasy Blood & Tissue is preferred (26). Multilocus sequence typing (MLST), Pulse-field gel electrophoresis (PFGE), DNA sequencing, MREJ (SSC*mec* right extremity junction) and *Staphylococcal* cassette chromosome (SCC*mec)* typing are also performed for the detection of MRSA (27) (28). Several strategies for the treatment of MRSA have been implicated, several guidelines or policies have been published for the prevention and control of MRSA by governmental, public health and some of the professional organization (29).

The current review is trying to address the problems of MRSA infections associated with various hospitals with a special emphasis on their drug-resistant profile.

2

GENERAL DESCRIPTION AND IDENTIFICATION OF *Staphylococcus aureus*

Historical perspective

In the year 1884, Anton Rosenbach provided the description that the genus *Staphylococcus* was divided into two species *i.e. Staphylococcus aureus* ("golden staph", for the golden colonies grown on bacterial media) and *Staphylococcus albus* (white colonies). In the year 1885, a third species *Staphylococcus citreus* was added by Passet (30).

Definition of the genus

Staphylococcus is one of the most important bacteria which is responsible for causing human disease and death. It also leads to cause hospital-acquired infection (31). *Staphylococci* are mainly characterized by gram-positive, non-spore former, non-motile microorganisms. The cells are spherically shaped from 5 to 1.5μm in diameter. They occur as single cocci, in pairs, and in chains. The cell can also divide into more than one plane and can form irregular clusters like bunches of grapes. They are basically catalase positive, oxidase negative, facultatively anaerobic and are often uncapsulated (32). *Staphylococcus* is susceptible to furazolidone (100μg) and resistant to bacitracin (0.04 units) at a minimum level. Based on the lysis mechanism they are susceptible to lysostaphin and are relatively resistant to lysozyme (30).
Staphylococcus is composed of 37 species, out of which 16 *S. aureus* species were found in humans. Among those species, the most virulent *S. aureus* and *S. lugudensis* were found in humans and *S. aureus* and *S. intermedius* were found in animals (33).

Habitat

S. aureus colonizes in the skin and mucosa of all animals, including mammals and birds (34). *S. aureus* demonstrated a preference for the anterior nares, especially in human mostly adults (35). It exists as a resident or as a transient member of the normal flora. The rate of the nasal carrier may vary from 10%-40% in both the hospital and the

Prevalence and Detection of Methicillin Resistant *Staphylococcus aureus* (MRSA)

community environment (36). The role of nasal carriage in *Staphylococcus aureus* infection has become a means of persistence and spread of multiresistant *S. aureus* especially MRSA (37).

Identification of *Staphylococcus aureus*
Cell morphology

The Gram stained cells observed are uniformly Gram-positive and appear spherical with an average diameter of 0.5-1.5μm (30). Cell wall deficient (L-form) cells were described for *S. aureus* (38). The cell wall of *S. aureus* consists of peptidoglycan with a molecule of a ribitol- teichoic acid. In most of the strains, of *S. aureus*, the peptidoglycan cell wall is over-laid with some surface proteins (39).

Cultural characteristics

The colonies of *Staphylococcus* species mostly grows in a diameter of 1-3 mm after an incubation period of 24 hours. *Staphylococcal* colonies are smooth, butyrous and possess a low convex profile with an entire edge. The pigmentation of the species is characterized when grown aerobically and the color of the colony changes from cream to gold. *S. aureus* tolerates the concentrations of sodium chloride that inhibit other bacteria and on Mannitol Salt Agar it forms yellow colonies of diameter 1mm surrounded by yellow medium due to acid formation. On MacConkey or Cysteine Lactose Electrolyte Deficient agar (CLED), it acquires the color of the indicator depending upon the strain on the basis of their fermentation capability to ferment lactose (40) (32).

There are different selective media for isolating *S. aureus*. These include phenyl ethyl alcohol agar, salt broth, mannitol salt agar, Columbia colistin nalidixic acid (CNA) agar, Baird-Parker agar base (30). Severe unusual morphology of *S. aureus* has been described that is significantly different from the normal colony which includes certain encapsulated strains (41), small colony variant (SCV) (30) and L-forms (38). The strain which showed SCV morphology was resistant to aminoglycosides. They are mostly isolated from infections such as cystic fibrosis or chronic osteomyelitis (42). When incubated on blood agar, *S. aureus* produces white colonies and shows β-hemolysis surrounding the colony (39).

Biochemical reactions

The most important test which is performed to test *S. aureus* is the coagulase test. This test distinguishe S. *aureus* from other *Staphylococci*, as they produce coagulase which non enzymatically binds to prothrombin, forming a complex that initiates the polymerization of fibrin (39). They also hydrolyze urea, reduces nitrates to nitrites,

Prevalence and Detection of Methicillin Resistant *Staphylococcus aureus* (MRSA)

methyl red and Voges-Proskauer test positive, indole test-negative, produce phosphatase, they ferment a number of sugars producing acid but no gas (40) (30,32).

S. aureus also produces extracellular proteins, which are harmful to the tissues of man and animals. Some of these include enzymes which are capable of degrading connective tissue (hyaluronidase), membranes and serum components (phospholipases and lipases), nucleic acids (deoxyribonuclease), proteins (proteases) and a variety of esterases (sugar phosphates and cholesteryl esters). They also produce another group of extracellular proteins which is known as the exotoxins. These exotoxins are the membrane-damaging proteins cytolysins, hemolysins toxins (43). These extracellular proteins convert the host tissues into nutrients. These nutrients are used by the bacteria for their growth. The bacterial strains also produce some additional exoproteins such as toxic shock syndrome toxin-1 (TSST-1), the *Staphylococcal* enterotoxins (SEA, SEB, SECn, SED, SEE, SEG, SEH, and SEI), the exfoliative toxins (ETA and ETB) and leukocidin. Each of these toxins is known to have potent effects on cells of the immune system, but many of them have other biological effects as well (44).

3

MRSA INFECTION AND ANTIBIOTIC RESISTANCE

Clinical manifestation

The bacterial infection begins with the colonization of the target tissues by *S. aureus*. They mainly colonize the anterior nares. The infection results when the bacteria interacts directly or indirectly (through toxins) with the host (35).

S. aureus causes a wide range of infections like minor skin infection, such as pimples, impetigo, boils, cellulitis, folliculitis, scalded skin syndrome, and abscesses, to life-threatening diseases such as pneumonia, endocarditis, toxic shock syndrome, bacteremia, and sepsis and they can be divided into the community as well as hospital-acquired infections (30).

Community-acquired infections

1) Toxin-mediated disease : *Staphylococcal* scalded skin syndrome, *Staphylococcal* food poisoning, and Toxic shock syndrome (45).
2) Skin and soft tissue infection : Some skin lesions induced by *S. aureus* such as exudate or an abscess. Some of the infection are classified according to their anatomic structure include Impetigo, Folliculitis, Furuncles, Cellulitis (45).
3) Bone and Joint sepsis: Primary septic arthritis and osteomyelitis are caused by *S. aureus* (46).
4) Bacteremia and endocarditis: *S. aureus* bacteremia is nosocomially acquired infection which is associated with intravenous device-related infection. Endocarditis on a native valve is one of the most severe infections of *S. aureus* bacteremia (47).

Nosocomial or Hospital-acquired infections

Some of the hospital-acquired infections include surgical wound infection, ventilator-associated pneumonia, infection associated with a prosthetic material such as CSF shunts, vascular grafts and prosthetic joints (48).

Prevalence and Detection of Methicillin Resistant *Staphylococcus aureus* (MRSA)

Antibiotics resistance in *S. aureus*

After the introduction of penicillin in medicine in the early 1940's, penicillin-resistant *S. aureus* strains have emerged. The percentage of penicillin-resistant strains has risen to 75-95% with the highest rate. The most of these strains were found among the hospital strains (30). Most of the penicillin-resistant *Staphylococcal* strains produce β-lactamase which hydrolyzes the β-lactam ring. The β-lactamase genes (*blaZ*) are found on the class II plasmids and *bla*Z genes have two regulatory genes, the antirepressor *bla*R1 and the repressor *bla*I (49).

Methicillin Resistance

Methicillin-resistant *Staphylococcus aureus* (MRSA) was first discovered by the British scientists in the early 1960's and it is now regarded as a major hospital-acquired pathogen. MRSA is resistant to many antibiotics such as methicillin, amoxicillin, penicillin, and oxacillin (50). The methicillin-resistant strain which was isolated from the hospitalized patients in Britain were multiple antibiotic resistant, belonged to the phage group III (51).

The infection associated with MRSA includes endovascular infections, skin, and soft-tissue infections, septic arthritides, sepsis, osteomyelitis, and endocarditis which are resistant to certain antibiotics such as lincosamides, aminoglycosides, macrolides and all the beta-lactam antimicrobials (52). In the mid-1970's, the large number of hospital-acquired outbreaks were recorded due to infection of MRSA (30). Many of these outbreaks have been caused by a single epidemic strain that was transferred to hospitals by the patients. MRSA is now responsible for around 30% or more *S. aureus* infections (30).

The hospital associated MRSA are resistant to nearly all the beta-lactam antibiotics. The microorganisms are responsible for nosocomial infections and their treatment can be effectively challenging. In the year 2011, a new type of *mec*C bearing MRSA was recognized. Mostly the strains of MRSA carry the *mec*A gene, which resides on genetic element known as the *Staphylococcal* chromosomal cassette *mec* (SCC*mec*). The SCC*mec* gene codes for the PBP2a (penicillin-binding protein) and this protein interferes with the cell walls of *S. aureus* with the effects of beta-lactam antibiotics. It almost shows resistant to nearly all the beta-lactam antibiotics which include semi-synthetic penicillins such as oxacillin, cloxacillin or methicillin (53).

In the late 1950s at Denmark, an operation of the *Staphylococcal* disease has been performed at the Statens Serum Institute by the National Surveillance System. *S. aureus* which was isolated from blood cultures has been preserved since 1959 (54). From 1988

Prevalence and Detection of Methicillin Resistant *Staphylococcus aureus* (MRSA)

the infectious and colony forming MRSA were collected and stored for the further experimental purpose. By the mid-1970s the hospital-acquired MRSA has been reduced due to the implementation of strict infection control measures but in the recent year 2016, a number of cases of MRSA infection in Denmark have been identified by National Surveillance System (54).

In most of the areas of the USA and some European countries, around >50% of *S. aureus* shows resistance to methicillin. This shows that MRSA has been a widespread between different countries and across the continent (55). In Japan, the MRSA isolated from skin samples has been shown to vary from 10 to 20% (56).

Vancomycin resistance

Vancomycin is a glycopeptide antibiotic that was introduced in the mid-1950s. Clinically the first vancomycin-intermediate *Staphylococcus aureus* (VISA) strain (Mu50) with a vancomycin minimum inhibitory concentration (MIC) of 8 mg/L was isolated in 1996 (57,58). Vancomycin primarily targets the D-ala-D-ala subunit of the gram-positive cell wall. They bind to its target (D-ala-D-ala) and do not bind to the D-ala-D-ala side chains at the cytoplasmic membrane that is actively involved in the formation of cross-links. This leads to cell death by inhibiting cell wall crosslinking (58,59).

4

TYPES OF METHICILLIN RESISTANT *Staphylococcus aureus* (MRSA)

1. Hospital-acquired MRSA (HA-MRSA)

The source of Hospital-acquired MRSA infection is basically from the medical facilities which include hospitals, nursing homes, laboratory *etc*. The infection spread through direct contact with an infected wound of a person or through contaminated hands. Infection can also spread when coming into contact with poorly sanitized surgical instruments. Hospital-acquired MRSA causes severe infections include blood infections, pneumonia *etc* (61,62).

Symptoms of HA-MRSA

Symptoms are generally rashes, headaches, chills, fever, fatigue, cough, muscles aches, shortness of breath, chest pain *etc*. It also causes some serious complications, such as urinary tract infections, pneumonia, and sepsis (63,64).

2. Community-acquired MRSA (CA-MRSA)

The CA-MRSA infections were transmitted through direct contact with an infected person or through close personal contact with an infected person. Poor hygiene condition, improper hand-washing can cause the infection (65,66).

Symptoms of CA-MRSA

Skin infection was mainly caused by CA-MRSA. The areas of the body parts with increased hair were mostly infected. The areas mostly the skins which were damaged due to cuts, scratched or rubbed were vulnerable to infection as they the biggest barriers to infection. Swollen of skin, painful bump surrounded by an area of redness and warmth which is known as cellulitis is seen. Pus and fluids were drained off from the area affected (67,68).

5

MECHANISM OF METHICILLIN RESISTANT IN MRSA

Benzylpenicillin (penicillin G) is a β-lactam antibiotic that was used for the treatment of *S. aureus* infection before 1950. But by the late 1950s, *S. aureus* shows resistant to benzyl-penicillin. The resistant strains of these antibiotics produce an enzyme known as β-lactamases which inactivate the β-lactam. To prevent the β-lactamase hydrolysis an effort was made to synthesize penicillin derivatives, which was achieved in 1959, with the synthesis of an antibiotic named as methicillin. Methicillin has a phenol group of benzylpenicillin which is distributed with the methoxy group. The presence of methoxy group produces a steric hindrance around the amide bond which reduces the affinity for *Staphylococcal* β-lactamases. Unfortunately, as soon as methicillin was used clinically, a methicillin-resistant *S. aureus* (MRSA) strain was isolated. This resistance was not due to the β-lactamase production but they express an additional penicillin-binding protein (PBP2a) which shows resistant to the action of antibiotics (69). The structure of Benzylpenicillin and Methicillin is showed in **"Fig 1"**.

Benzylpenicillin (reference: Stapleton *et. al.,* 2007)

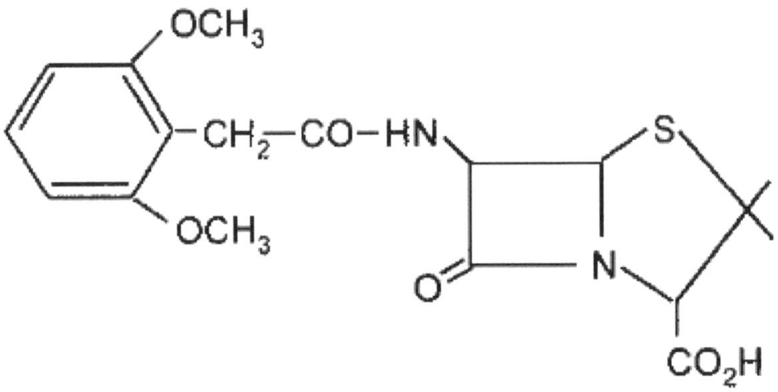

Prevalence and Detection of Methicillin Resistant *Staphylococcus aureus* (MRSA)

Methicillin **(reference: Stapleton *et. al.,* 2007)**

Figure 1: The chemical structure of β-lactam antibiotics (a) Benzylpenicillin and (b) Methicillin

*mec*A gene

*mec*A is a biomarker gene which is resistant to methicillin and other β-lactam antibiotics. It is the part of the genetic element found in the MRSA strains. The *mec*A gene must be localized in the *Staphylococcus* chromosome. The *mec*A gene encodes the penicillin-binding protein 2a (PBP2a). This enzyme is necessary for cross-linkage of peptidoglycan chain (70). There are three types of *mec* elements, which comprise the *mec*A and the divergently transcribed regulatory element *mec*R1-*mec*I. The *mec*R1 is a transmembrane β-lactam sensing protein which acts as a signal transducer in the β-lactam induction of *mec*A. They also carry a cytoplasmic oriented Zn-peptidase motif. The *mec*I gene act as a repressor of *mec*A which shows homology to the β-lactamase repressor *Bla*I (71). *Bla*I and *Bla*R1 were two regulatory genes encoded by the structural gene *Bla*Z.

The *mec*I and *mec*R1 are the two regulatory genes which were under the control of *mec*A gene **"Fig 2"**. The *mec*I gene functions as a repressor and binds to the *mec*A promoter. *mec*R1 initiates a signal transduction cascade in the presence of a β-lactam antibiotic, that leads to transcriptional activation of *mec*A. *mec*R1 cleaves the *mec*I which bound to the operator region of *mec*A promoter that inhibits the production of PBP2a protein. The inhibition of protein PBP2a resulted in the β-lactam antibiotic that cannot bind to the PBP2a protein. Therefore, the synthesis of the cell wall is able to proceed. The regulatory genes *bla*I and *bla*R1 also regulate *mec*A expression (72).

The fem genes (factors essential for methicillin resistance), also plays an important role in peptidoglycan strands crosslinking and contribute to the heterogeneous expression of methicillin resistance (73). There is no homologous of *mec*A gene exists in the methicillin-susceptible *Staphylococcus aureus* and it is assumed that *mec*A gene was

Prevalence and Detection of Methicillin Resistant *Staphylococcus aureus* (MRSA)

acquired from one of the coagulase-negative *Staphylococcal* species (74). A homologous *mec*A gene was observed in the *S. sciuri* which showed 88% the amino acid similarity to the *mec*A gene of MRSA (75).

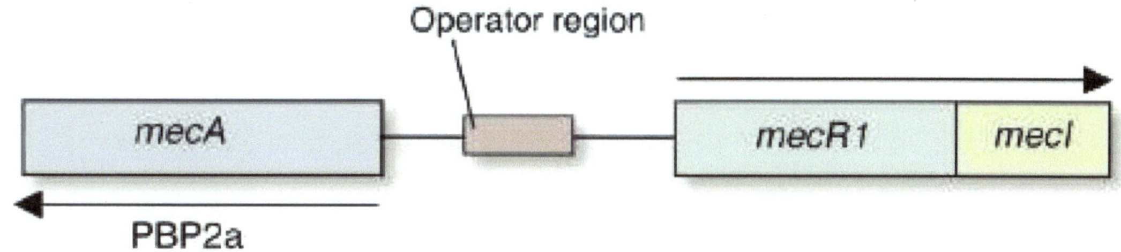

Figure 2: Synthesis of PBP2a protein by *mec*A gene (reference: Lowy *et. al.*, 2003).

6

PREVALENCE OF *Staphylococcus aureus*

There is a continuous need to assess the epidemiology of MRSA and its infections. It is extremely imperative to evaluate and monitor the infection as it gives an idea of success or failure of infection control program. Considering that different MRSA infection is seen in different countries and hospitals worldwide.

An estimated report shows that 2 billion healthy peoples carry *Staphylococcus aureus* up to 53 million peoples are thought to carry Methicillin-resistant *Staphylococcus aureus* (MRSA). *S. aureus* is considered as a dreadful pathogen because it causes severe infections and tremendously spread by metastatic foci. The potential sites for infection of *S. aureus* are commonly the nostrils, skin, perineum, respiratory tract, open wounds, and urinary tract. The estimated fatality rates of MRSA infections ranges from 20% to 50% (76).

The National scenario

In a tertiary care hospital, Mamata Medical College, Khammam, Telangana a total of 210 strains of *Staphylococci* were collected from different clinical samples like pus, sputum, blood, urine and body fluids from patients of both admitted cases inpatients department (IPD) and outpatients departments (OPD) from February 2013 to December 2015. Out of the 210 *Staphylococcal* isolates, 165 (78.57%) were founded as *Staphylococcus aureus* and 45 (21.43%) were founded as coagulase-negative *Staphylococci*. Among the 165 *Staphylococcus aureus* isolates, 53 (32.12%) isolates were found to be MRSA. The numbers of isolates were highest in wound swab and pus and were least in body fluids and blood. The overall percentage of MRSA from OPD and IPD is 30.18% and 69.82% respectively. Out of 210 *S. aureus* isolates, 102 isolated from male and 108 from female of which 53 were identified as MRSA. In 53 MRSA isolates, the 21 were present in male and 32 were in the female. In this study, the comparison of MRSA between IPD and OPD were 69.82% (37) and 30.18% (16) respectively. An antibiotic sensitivity test was also performed for the different antibiotics like Penicillin (10U), Gentamycin (10µg), Erythromycin (15µg), Ciprofloxacin (5µg), Linezolid (30µg), Amikacin (30µg),

Prevalence and Detection of Methicillin Resistant *Staphylococcus aureus* (MRSA)

Ampicillin (10µg), Cotrimoxazole (35µg), Cefotaxime (30µg), Vancomycin (30µg) and Cefoxitin (30µg) (77).

In Shah Medical College and Hospital, Surendra nagar, Gujarat a total of 200 strains of *S. aureus* have been isolated from various clinical specimens of different patients during the period of September 2009 to December 2010. Most of the MRSA has been isolated from the wound and cutaneous specimens (51.22%), followed by urine (28.05%), sputum (15.85%) and blood (3.66%). This study results that, out of 200 isolates of *S. aureus*, 117 (58.5%) were methicillin resistant and 110 (94.02%) were found to be multidrug resistant. Among the 117 MRSA strains, 80.49 % were resistant to cefaclor, 86.59% ciprofloxacin, 79.27% to erythromycin and 81.71% to cephalexin. The study prevails that vancomycin was the most effective drug as the MRSA isolates were sensitive to it. The 93.90% MRSA isolates were found to be sensitive to linezolid and 91.46% were sensitive to teicoplanin. Some of the isolates of MRSA (82.91%) were also found as the co-producers of β-lactamase (78).

From January 2007 to February 2008, a case study was performed in a tertiary care hospital in Assam. From various clinical samples, a total of 276 *S. aureus* strains were isolated. Antibiotic susceptibility pattern was performed by modified Kirby Bauer disc diffusion method against the following antibiotics: Oxacillin (1µg), Penicillin (10µg), Cephalexin (30µg), Gentamicin (10µg) Amikacin (30µg), Trimethoprim/ Sulfamethoxazole (1.25/23.75µg), Ciprofloxacin (5µg), Erythromycin (15µg) and Clindamycin (2µg). Out of the 276 isolates, 96 (34.78%) were found to be methicillin-resistant. Most of the MRSA has been isolated from pus/wound swabs (46.67%) followed by sputum/throat swab (42.86%) (79).

During January to December 2006, a cross-sectional study was conducted in a tertiary care hospital of Sikkim. A total of 827 clinical specimens were collected from different departments of Central Referral Hospital. The 196 nasal swabs were obtained from healthcare workers of the hospital. The antibiotic susceptibility test was performed by the Kirby Bauer Disc Diffusion method against the antibiotics-penicillin G (10 units), ampicillin (10 µg), erythromycin (15 µg), tetracycline (30 µg), gentamicin (10 µg), netilmicin (30 µg), vancomycin (30 µg), ciprofloxacin (5 µg), and imipenem (10 µg). Out of the 152 isolates of *S. aureus*, 41 from carrier screening samples and 111 from clinical specimens were found as methicillin resistance. In this study, it was found that MRSA positivity among males was significantly higher than females (19).

The study was carried out in a teaching hospital at Mangalore, South India from June 2007 to 2008. 237 clinical samples of *S. aureus* were isolated from various samples of blood, urine, pus *etc* from the patient of the hospital. The isolates from pus and wound

Prevalence and Detection of Methicillin Resistant *Staphylococcus aureus* (MRSA)

swabs were in majority that is 181 (76.3%) followed by urine, respiratory specimens, blood and body fluids. The Antibiotic sensitivity testing was performed by disc diffusion (Kirby– Bauer) method for the following antibiotics- Amikacin (30μgm), Ciprofloxacin (5μgm), Chloramphenicol (30 μgm), Clindamycin (2 μgm), Gentamicin (10 μgm), Erythromycin (15 μmg), Netilmicin (30 μgm), Penicillin (10 units), Rifampicin (5 μgm), and Vancomycin (30 μmg). The erythromycin (15 μgm) disc was placed at a distance of 15 mm (edge-to-edge) from clindamycin (2 μgm) disc on a Mueller–Hinton agar plate previously inoculated with 0.5 McFarland bacterial suspensions. The methicillin resistance was documented in 69 (29.1%) out of 237 isolates (80).

Total of 235 *Staphylococcus* isolates was recovered from the inpatients at Government Medical College and Hospital Anantapur, India during the period from June to December 2007. The clinical isolate included in this study was pus (55 isolates), urine (64), wound swabs (53), Nasal and Ear swabs (38) and blood (25). The antibiotic susceptibility pattern of all the specimens was determined by modified Kirby Bauer disc diffusion method against the following antibiotics: Penicillin (60 μg), Oxacillin (1μg), Gentamicin (10 μg), Erythromycin (15 μg), Cotrimoxazole (25 μg), Ciprofloxacin (5 μg) and Vancomycin (30 μg). Out of the 235 isolates were tested in which 117 were reported as methicillin-resistant *S. aureus* (81).

The study was conducted in the Department of Microbiology, Gajra Raja Medical College, Gwalior from April 2010 to March 2013. During the period of three years, a total of 5,259 cases of surgical site infection were included in the study and two pus samples were collected from each patient with sterile swabs. The antibiotic susceptibility test was performed against all these antibiotics including Ciprofloxacin (5μg), Co-trimoxazole (10μg), Gentamicin (10μg), Amikacin (30μg), Clindamycin (2μg), Erythromycin (30μg), Chloramphenicol (30μg), Cephalexin (10μg), Vancomycin (30μg), Linezolid (30μg), Penicillin (30μg), Amoxicillin (30μg), Amoxiclav (10μg), Cefuroxime (30μg), and Cefotaxime (30μg). In this study total 410 (27.96%) isolates were identified as MRSA (82).

Between December 2001 and March 2002, in AIIMS New Delhi, 2080 samples were received from surgical wound infection. The samples were cultured on Blood Agar and MacConkey agar plates. 800 (38%) were found as positive *S. aureus* 60 (75%) were found as coagulase-negative *Staphylococcus* and 112 (44%) were found to be resistant to methicillin, out of 2080 isolates. The isolates were resistant to the following antibiotics: Vancomycin (100%), Rifampicin (62%), Teicoplanin (56%), Amikacin (31%), Ciprofloxacin (16%), Cefuroxime (11%), Amoxicillin (6.25%). Out of 112 MRSA, 66 isolates were reported as positive β-lactamase and 46 were detected as negative β-lactamase (18).

Prevalence and Detection of Methicillin Resistant *Staphylococcus aureus* (MRSA)

A study was performed in Guru Tegh Bahadur Hospital, Delhi shows that out of 319 samples which were collected from nasal swabs from some of the healthy person attending a baby clinic, 94 (29.4%) isolates were found to be *S. aureus*. Out of those 94 isolates, 17 (18.1%) were found resistant to oxacillin and some of the strains also showed resistant to clindamycin (20). The data were summarized in **"Table 1"** and **"Fig 3"**.

Table 1: Resistance pattern of MRSA to antibiotics in Indian hospitals

Antibiotics	Number of MRSA isolates in different studies							Total (mean representation)
	Among *et. al.,* 2017	Pandya *et. al.,* 2014	Saikia *et. al.,* 2008	Tsering *et. al.,* 2011	Khadri *et. al.,* 2010	Ranjan *et. al.,* 2013	Saxena *et. al.,* 2003	
Van	0	0	0	59	0	100	0	159
Lin	15	7	0	0	0	100	0	115
Cef	32	7	0	0	0	0	0	39
Chl	0	29	0	0	0	44	0	73
Clin	0	37	43.75	0	0	56	4	140.75
Dox	0	43	0	0	0	0	0	43
Amp	42	40	0	14	0	0	0	96
Gen	33	44	12.5	0	65	42.4	13	209.9
Tet	0	47	0	16	54	0	0	117
Clox	0	3	0	0	0	0	0	3
Ami	32	0	21.38	0	0	90.0	0	143.58
Lev	0	78	0	0	0	0	0	78
Ery	33	93	18	12	74	32	9	271.75
Cot	17	0	0	0	73	30.3	0	120.3
Ceph	0	96	0	0	62	74	0	232
Cip	45	101	12.5	23	36	36.2	12	265.7
Pen	53	0	0	21	89	0	0	163
Oxa	0	0	0	0	89	0	0	89

(Antibiotics: Van- Vancomycin, Lin- Linezolid, Cef- Cefotaxime, Chl-Chloramphenicol, Clin- Clindamycin, Dox- Doxycynin, Amp- Ampicillin, Gen- Gentamycin, Tet- Tetracycline, Clox- Cloxacillin, Ami- Amikacin, Lev- Levofloxacin, Ery- Erythromycin, Cot- Cotrimoxazole, Ceph- Cephalexin, Cip- Ciprofloxacin, Pen- Penicillin, Oxa- Oxacillin).

Prevalence and Detection of Methicillin Resistant *Staphylococcus aureus* (MRSA)

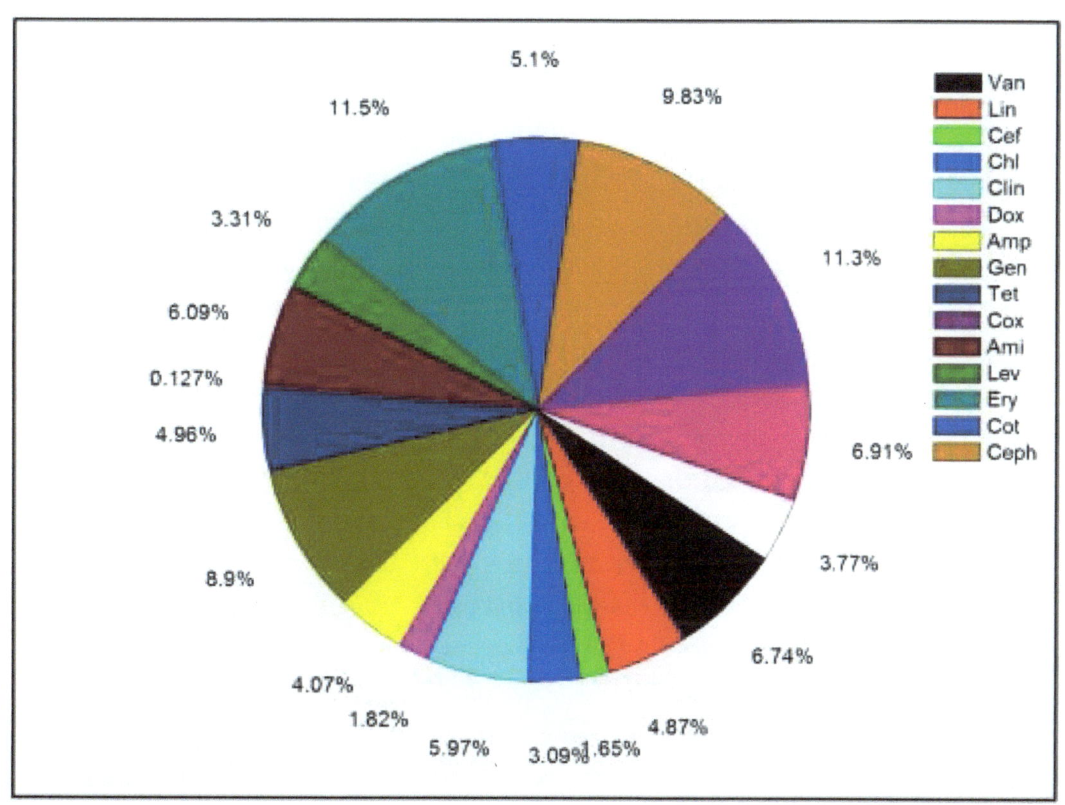

Figure 3: Graphical representation of the MRSA antibiogram in Indian scenario

The International scenario

This study was performed in the Universal College of Medical Sciences Teaching Hospital, Bhairahawa, Western Nepal during June 2005 and July 2007. A total of 162strains of *S. aureus* were isolated from various clinical specimens from different patients. 112 (69.1%) isolates were found to be resistant to methicillin and 71% of MRSA isolates out of 162 isolates were reported from pus swabs or aspirates. Out of the 112 MRSA isolates, 37 (33.1%) were from community-acquired infections and 75 (66.9%) were from nosocomial infections. About 45 (41%) were multi-drug resistant in which most (22%) of the isolates were from urine samples. Antibiotic susceptibility test shows a very high degree of resistance against these following antibiotics: Penicillin (100%), Amoxicillin (91.8%), Ampicillin (90%), Cotrimoxazole (72.7%), and Cephalexin (66.03%); lower degrees of resistance were also observed with Amikacin (40%) Ciprofloxacin (45.8%), and Norfloxacin (43.4%) (17).

Prevalence and Detection of Methicillin Resistant *Staphylococcus aureus* (MRSA)

In a tertiary surgical hospital in Benghazi, Libya, a case study was investigated on the prevalence of MRSA strains and their sensitivity patterns against various antibiotics. The clinical sample was isolated from the patients who admitted to the hospital specimens of pus from abscesses wound swabs, blood, cerebrospinal fluid, central venous line tips, endotracheal tube tips and urine catheter tips were included in this study. The further study was conducted at the Microbiology Laboratory at Aljala Surgical and Trauma Hospital, Benghazi, Libya, from April to July 2007. Total 200 isolates were reported from different clinical samples in which 62 (31%) were MRSA. The MRSA was detected in 31.8% (28/88) from females and 30.4% (34/112) from males. It was observed that 20.3% (26/128) of *S. aureus* was from patients with skin and soft tissue infections in the form of abscesses, cellulitis and diabetic foot: 54% (27/50) from patients with surgical wound infection; 40% (6/15) from patients who underwent invasive procedures in the ICU and 50% (2/4) from patients with chronic orthopedic disease in the form of chronic osteomyelitis and septic arthritis. The antibiotic susceptibility test was performed using disc-diffusion method which showed the resistance pattern of 62 patients with MRSA were as follows: resistance to Vancomycin was observed in 11 (17.7%) cases, resistance to Ciprofloxacin 21 (33.9%) cases, resistance to Chloramphenicol 24 (38.7%) cases, fusidic acid resistance 26 (41.9%) cases and resistance to Erythromycin 29 (46.8%) cases (16).

This study was based on prospective and observation of the patients with skin and soft tissue infections in an urban public hospital of California from October 2003 to February 2004. During a period of 5 months, 137 patients were enrolled. The infections types consisted of 66 deep abscesses, 20 superficial skin abscesses (furuncles), 18 cases of pure cellulitis and 32 cases of other types of infection such as ulcer and wound infections. Out of 119 infection-site cultures, 79(66.4%) isolates grew as *S. aureus* of which 61 were MRSA (83).

In the year 2017 in Tanzania, a total of 258 patients were included in this study. This study aimed to determine the rate of MRSA and the associated risk factors among the patients. Nasal swabs were collected. Out of the 258 patients enrolled, 89 (34.5%) were colonized with *S. aureus* and out of the 22 (24.7%) were the carriers of MRSA. The antibiotic susceptibility test was carried out using Kirby Bauer's disc diffusion method according to the guidelines of clinical and laboratory standards institute (CLSI) 2015. The following antibiotic disks were used: Penicillin G (10U), Kanamycin (30 µg), Gentamicin (10 µg), Erythromycin (15 µg), Clindamycin (2 µg), Ciprofloxacin (5 µg), Linezolid (30 µg) and Mupirocin (5 µg). Most of the *S. aureus* isolates 85(95.5%) were resistant to Penicillin. The 14.6%, 11.2%, 11.2%, 3.4%, and 1.1% were resistant to Gentamycin, Ciprofloxacin, Kanamycin, Linezolid, and Mupirocin. Out of the 258 patients, 150 (58.1%) were females. This study observed a high proportion of MRSA

Prevalence and Detection of Methicillin Resistant *Staphylococcus aureus* (MRSA)

(24.7%) among patients who were colonized with *S. aureus* (84). The data were summarizing in **"Table 2"** and **"Fig 4".**

Table 2: Resistance pattern of MRSA to antibiotics in international hospitals

Antibiotics	MRSA (%)				Total (mean representation)
	Tiwari *et. al.*,2007	Buzaid *et. al.*, 2004	Fraze *et. al.*, 2005	Joachim *et. al.*, 2017	
Pen	100	0	0	63	163
Norf	43.4	26	0	0	69.4
Kan	56.5	0	0	0	56.5
Ery	68.7	29	3.6	0	101.3
Clox	100	0	0	0	100
Amp	90	0	0	0	90
Amo	91.8	0	0	0	91.8
Tet	52.3	0	85.7	0	138
Tri/Sulfa	72.7	0	100	0	172.7
Cip	45.8	21	94.3	8	169.1
Ceph	66.03	0	0	2	68.03
Ami	40	0	0	0	40
Cefa	57.6	0	0	0	57.6
Van	0	11	100	0	111
Chl	0	24	0	0	24
Lin	0	0	0	2	2

(Antibiotics: Pen- Penicillin, Norf- Norfloxacin, Kan- Kanamycin, Ery- Erythromycin, Clox- Cloxacillin, Amp- Ampicillin, Amo-Amoxicillin, Tet- Tetracycline, Tri- Trimethoprim, Sulfa- Sulfamethoxazole, Cip- Ciprofloxacin, Cep- Cephalexin, Ami- Amikacin, Cef- Cefazolin, Van- Vancomycin, Chl- Chloramphenicol, Lin- Linezolid).

Prevalence and Detection of Methicillin Resistant *Staphylococcus aureus* (MRSA)

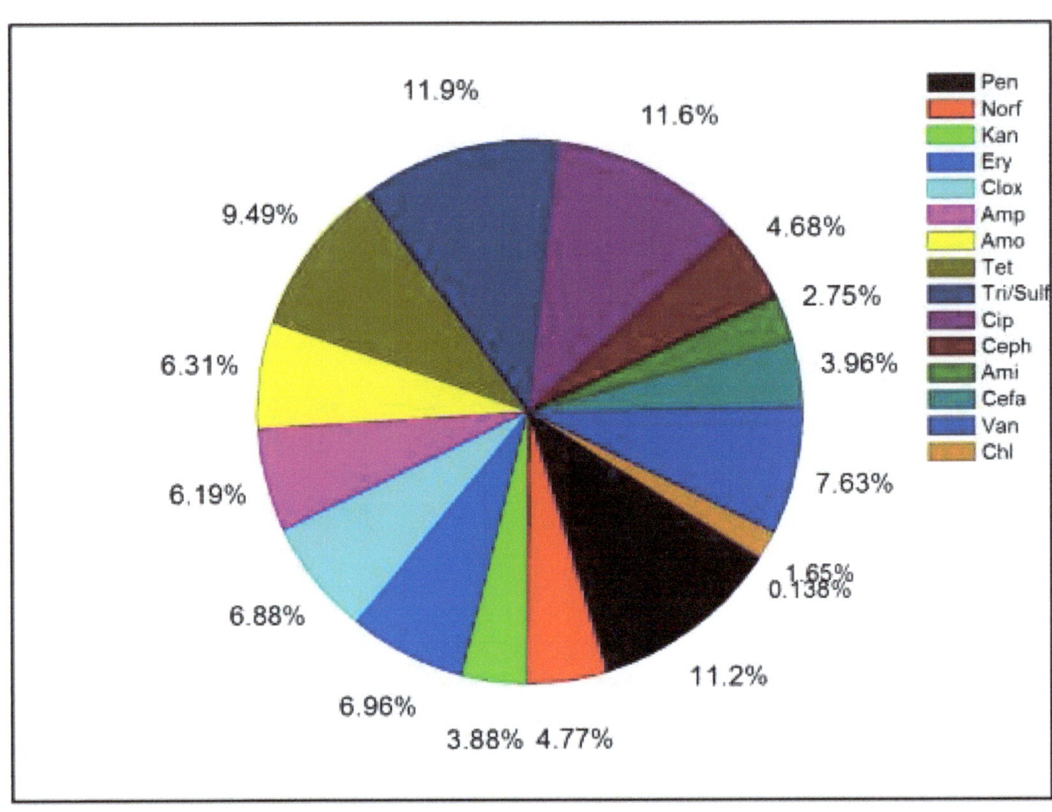

Figure 4: Graphical representation of MRSA isolates in International scenario

7

PHENOTYPIC METHODS FOR DETECTION OF MRSA

Phenotypic Methods

Different phenotypic methods are performed in the clinical laboratories such as oxacillin agar diffusion test, oxacillin and cefoxitin disc diffusion test, determination of minimum inhibitory concentration (MIC) *etc.* The expression of the resistant strains was affected by various conditions such as the difference in medium (media), temperature, size of the inoculum and concentration of NaCl in the medium (85). The phenotypic methods for the detection of MRSA strains follow the guidelines published in standardized clinical and laboratory standards Institute (CLSI, 2017) (86) (87) (88).

Oxacillin and Methicillin susceptibility

The antibiotic susceptibility test to methicillin was performed by the disk-diffusion method. The isolates of *Staphylococcus aureus* were cultured in 5% blood agar and incubated for 24 hours at 35°C temperature. The colonies observed on the blood agar plates were suspended in a saline solution to check for turbidity (concentration of a bacterial solution) equivalent to 0.5 on the McFarland scale (10^8CFU/ml). When turbidity reached to required concentration than with the help of a sterile swab, the bacterial suspension was seeded on the Mueller-Hinton agar plates. After completion of the seeding, cefoxitin disk (30mcg) were placed on the surface of an agar plate with the help of tweezer and result for the zone of inhibition were observed after 24-hour incubation (89) (90) (91). The methicillin-resistance was also determined by using 1μg of Oxacillin and 30μg of Cefoxitin. The Kirby Bauer disc diffusion methods were followed and the plates were incubated at 35°C for 24 hours (86) (24).

The Cefoxitin Disc Diffusion Test

Mueller-Hinton agar is used in cefoxitin disc diffusion method by using a 30 μg disc. Zone of inhibition was measured, a zone diameter of ≤ 21 mm was reported as methicillin-resistant a diameter of ≥ 22 mm was considered as methicillin sensitive (22) (86).

Prevalence and Detection of Methicillin Resistant *Staphylococcus aureus* (MRSA)

MIC Determination

1) Agar Dilution Method
2) Broth- Microdilution method
3) Macro dilution method
4) E- test

Procedure of Agar Dilution Method

The agar dilution test was performed with Mueller Hinton Agar/broth with 2% NaCl and MIC testing was performed with oxacillin. A peptone water culture of *S. aureus* corresponding to 0.5 McFarland turbidity is used as the inoculum. They are then inoculated either with multiple inoculators as spots or with a wire loop calibrated to deliver 0.001ml spread over a small area. The culture should be diluted to contain 10^5 to 10^6 organisms per ml. The Agar/broth was incubated for 24 hours at 33-35°C. The antibiotic concentration of the plate showing $\geq$ 99% inhibition is taken as the MIC for the microorganism (92) (93).

Oxacillin MIC $\leq$ 2 µg/ml – susceptible> 2 µg/ml- resistant

Broth Microdilution Method

This method is called "microdilution" because it involves the use of small volumes of broth dispensed in sterile, plastic microdilution trays that have round or conical bottom wells. Each well should contain 0.1 mL of broth. This test uses double-strength Mueller-Hinton broth, 4X strength antibiotic solutions prepared as serial two-fold dilutions and the test organism at a concentration of 2×10^6/ml. In the 96 well plate, 100µl of double strength Muller Hinton broth, 50µl each of the antibiotics dilutions and the organism suspension are mixed and incubated at 35°C for 18-24 hours. The lowest concentration showing inhibition of growth will be considered the MIC of the organism (94,95).

Broth Macrodilution Method

The 13×100 mm sterile test tube was used to conduct this test. A minimum final volume of 1 mL of each dilution is needed for the test. The test uses double strength Muller Hinton broth, antibiotics solution prepared as serial two-fold dilution and the test organisms at a concentration of 5×10^5/ml. Within 15 minutes after the inoculums have been standardized, 1ml of inoculums was added to each of the tube containing 1ml of antimicrobial agents in the dilution series and was mixed. This results in a 1:2 dilution of each antimicrobial concentration and a 1:2 dilution of the inoculums. The tubes were incubated at 35°C for 18-24 hours. The minimum inhibitory concentration was observed in each tube comparing the amount of growth in the wells or tubes containing the antimicrobial agent with the amount of growth in the growth-control wells or tubes (96,97).

Prevalence and Detection of Methicillin Resistant *Staphylococcus aureus* (MRSA)

E- test Method

E-test is also known as the epsilometer test is an exponential gradient testing methodology. The E refers to the Greek letter epsilon. The E test is a quantitative method for antimicrobial testing susceptibility testing which applies both the diffusion of the antibiotic and the dilution of the antibiotic into the medium. On a thin inert carrier strip, a predefined stable antimicrobial gradient is present. The drug is released immediately when the E strip is applied to the inoculated agar plate. After the incubation, asymmetrical inhibition ellipse is produced on the agar plate. The intersection of the inhibitory zone edge and the carrier strip indicates the MIC value over a wide concentration range with inherent accuracy and precision (98) (99).

Agar Screening Method

In this method, Mueller Hinton agar is used with 4% NaCl and 6μg/ml of oxacillin. The test organism inoculated as a spot corresponds to 0.5 Mc Farland turbidity standard and the plates are incubated at 35°C for 24 hours. Any growth in the agar plates is indicated as resistance (100) (101).

Antimicrobial susceptibility test

The Kirby Bauer disc diffusion method was used to detect the sensitivity of all *S. aureus* isolates and the interpretations were made according to the CLSI (2017) guidelines. For MRSA, cotrimoxazole (25 mg), clindamycin (10mg), erythromycin (15mg), ciprofloxacin (30mg), netilmicin (30mg), amikacin (10mg), linezolid (30mg), vancomycin (30mg), cotrimoxazole (25mg) were placed in different microbial agar plates and the zone of inhibition was observed which shows resistance against the antibiotics (102) (103).

Latex Agglutination

Latex agglutination test is based on detection of PBP2a (104) which is commercially available as a kit. This method involves the extraction of PBP2a from suspensions of colonies and is detected by agglutination with latex particles. These latex beads were coated with monoclonal antibodies to PBP2a. This test is very sensitive and specific with *S. aureus* (105,106) but may not be reliable for the colonies grown on media containing NaCl (107). This method requires no special equipment and is suitable for confirmation of resistance in clinical laboratories. The isolates producing a small amount of PBB2a give weak agglutination reactions. The reaction of PBP2a tends stronger when growth is induced in the presence of penicillin (107).

8

GENOTYPIC METHODS FOR DETECTION OF MRSA

Determination of *mec*A gene by Multiplex PCR method

PCR- based methods have been used routinely by different laboratories as their standard methods for detecting the *mec*A gene (108). Penicillin Binding Protein 2A (PBP2A) is coded by the *mec*A gene which is responsible for methicillin resistance. This *mec*A gene is highly conserved among the *Staphylococcal* species and the detection of this gene by PCR is considered as 'gold standard' of methicillin resistance against *Staphyloccocal* species (108) (24). The molecular diagnostic assay based on the detection of *mec*A gene encountered difficulty in discriminating MRSA from methicillin resistant coagulase negative *Staphylococcus* species as the *mec*A gene is widely distributed among *S. aureus* and in MR-CoNS (109).

Detection of resistance to Mupirocin

In this method, mupirocin resistance is tested against *mec*A gene by using 5µg discs (26). The *mup*A gene is used as a marker for high-level mupirocin resistance by PCR. The DNA was extracted from the *Staphylococcal* colonies after lysostaphin cell lysis for 30 minutes at 37°C by using the Qiagen kit DNeasy Blood & Tissue (110). A DNA sample of 3µl was used as a template in the PCR. Amplification is carried out through different repetitive cycles. The DNA fragments were separated by gel electrophoresis on 1.5% agarose gel stained with ethidium bromide (111–113).

Multilocus Sequence Typing (MLST)

MLST is a highly discriminatory method which is used for characterizing bacterial isolates. This is performed on the basis of the sequence of 450-bp internal fragments of the seven housekeeping genes (114) (27). Different sequences are assigned as distinct alleles for each of the gene fragments and each of the isolates is defined by the alleles present at each of the seven housekeeping loci. The isolates are unlikely to have an identical allelic profile as there are many alleles at each of the seven loci and this isolates can be assigned as the member of the same clone with the same allelic profile

Prevalence and Detection of Methicillin Resistant *Staphylococcus aureus* (MRSA)

(114,115). A major advantage of MLST is the ability to compare the data obtained from different studies via the internet. The data obtained from MLST can be used to determine basic questionnaires about the population and evolutionary biology of the bacterial species (116,117) (118).

Pulse field gel electrophoresis (PFGE)

The procedure was performed as described by Pfaller *et. al.,* (119). A bacterial suspension was mixed with 2% SeaPlague GTG agarose at 58°C. The suspension was allowed to solidify into plug molds at room temperature. The chromosomal DNA was prepared by using EC buffer (6mMTris-HCL, 1MNaCl, 0.1MEDTA, 0.5% Brij-58, 0.2% deoxycholate, 0.5% Sarkosyl), lysostaphin and proteinase K. The whole chromosomal DNA that embedded in agarose gel was digested with *Sma*I.The restriction fragments were separated by using a temperature-controlled CHEF DRII apparatus (Bio-Rad, Munich, Germany) at 6V/cm at a switching time that ranges from 5 to 60 seconds. The gels were stained with ethidium bromide and the fragments were visualized under UV transilluminator and then documented by using gel documentation system (MWG-Biotech) (120) (27).

The PFGE patterns were interpreted with slight modifications according to the criteria given by Tenover *et. al.,* (121). The isolates were distributed in three groups: (i) the isolates with identical banding pattern belongs to the same group; (ii) the isolates with differences in their PFGE patterns are designated as subtypes of a certain clone; and (iii) the isolates with more than three differences in the PFGE patterns are designated as different clone. For further results, the strains of different PFGE patterns were run again on different gels for identification. The visualization was done by analyzing it by using GelCompar software (Applied Maths, Kortrijk, Belgium) (122).

DNA Sequencing

Different primers were used to amplify and sequence the SRE junctions (MREJs) of various MRSA strains. The MREJ comprises the right extremity of SSC*mec*, the SCC*mec* integration site, and the orfX gene. The MREJ fragments to be sequenced were amplified on a PTC-200 thermocycler (MJ Research Inc, Watertown, Mass), using purified DNA (123). The Genomic DNAs were purified by using a Genome kit (Obiogene Inc., Carlsbad, Calif). The bacterial cells were resuspended in 250μl of a lysis solution containing 200μl of lysostaphin (Sigma Chemical Co., St. Louis, Mo.) per ml, 20mM Tris, 2mM EDTA, and 1.2% Triton X-100 and were incubated at 37°C for 30 min. The purified genomic DNA was diluted at a concentration of 1ng/μl in TE buffer (10mM Tris [pH 8.0], 1 mM EDTA)(124). Depending on the MRSA strain, amplification products having predicted sizes were recovered from an agarose gel stained 15 min with 0.02% methylene blue (Laboratoire MAT, Beauport, Quebec,

Prevalence and Detection of Methicillin Resistant *Staphylococcus aureus* (MRSA)

Canada) followed by washing in sterile distilled water for 15 min twice (125). The PCR products were recovered from the agarose gel using the QIAquick gel extraction kit (Qiagen Inc., Mississauga, Ontario, Canada). The amplicons were sequenced directly with the PRISM Ready Reaction DyeDeoxy Terminator Cycle Sequencing Kit using an Applied Biosystems 373A sequencer (Applied Biosystems, Foster City, Calif.) (126) (28).

SCC*mec* right extremity junction (MREJ) and SSC*mec* typing

The MREJ types of the MRSA strains were determined by sequence analysis or by examining the PCR amplification products generated by the multiplex PCR assay and standard agarose gel electrophoresis (127). The SCC*mec* types and subtypes of the MRSA strains were identified by using typing method (128). Primers *mec*IVc70 (5′-TGGGGTATTTTTATCTTCAACTC-3′) and *mec*IVc1079 (5′-TGGGATTTTAAAGCAGAATATCA-3′) were designed to identify SCC*mec* type IVc based on the SCC*mec* sequence of MRSA strain MR108 (128). Primers *mec*IVd26 (5′-ACGGGAGATTAGGAGATGTTAT-3′) and *mec*IVd307(5′-CAGCCATCAATTTTGTTTCACC-3′) were designed to identify SCC*mec* type IVd based on the SCC*mec* sequence of MRSA strain JCSC 4469 (GenBank accession number AB097677) (28).

9
STRATEGIES FOR TREATMENT OF MRSA

The Institute for Healthcare Improvement and The Association for Professionals in Infection Control and Epidemiology (APIC) have developed practical suggestions for implementation and monitoring several preventative measures specified in evidence-based guidelines (129).

Infrastructure requirement

Infrastructure requirement of MRSA prevention program includes:

I. An infection prevention and control (IPC) program which is staffed by a number of trained personnel to implement and sustain MRSA surveillance and prevention efforts without compromising other IPC activities (130).

II. Information technology system should be implemented to allow rapid notification to clinical staff and IPC personnel about new MRSA isolates, data collection needed to measure the outcome of MRSA-colonized patients (130).

III. Sufficient supplies for hand hygiene (eg. gowns and gloves), environmental cleaning and disinfection and other infection prevention should be implemented as the part of the MRSA control program (129).

IV. Appropriate education and training should be provided to direct care providers and other healthcare personnel (HCP), patients and visitors (130).

V. Adequate laboratory support (eg. sufficient staffing and resources for routine clinical testing and for additional testing when necessary, timely provision of relevant data to clinicians and the infection prevention program) (129).

Prevention of MRSA transmission and infection in all acute care hospitals
Conduct an MRSA risk assessment

1. The risk assessment should be attentive to two important factors:
   i. The opportunity for MRSA transmission.
   ii. Estimation of infection of MRSA carrier's patients.

2. The findings from the risk assessment should be used to develop the hospital's surveillance, prevention, and control plan and to develop goals to reduce MRSA transmission.
3. The risk assessment also provides a baseline for subsequent assessments and other data comparisons (131).
4. Implementation of MRSA monitoring program
    a) The MRSA monitoring program should have two goals that include the patient history must be ensured to provide a better prevention strategy according to the hospital policy and second to provide a mechanism for tracking the hospital-onset cases of MRSA for purpose of assessing transmission and infection (132).
5. To promote compliance with CDC or World Health Organization
    a) Hand hygiene is the fundamental strategy for the prevention of pathogen transmission in healthcare facilities.
    b) Patients-to-patient transmission of MRSA commonly occurs through transient colonization of the hands of HCP. Therefore, efforts should be made to improve the hand hygiene practices (133).
6. Ensure cleaning and disinfection of equipment and the environment
    a) MRSA contaminates the patient's environment (eg, overbed tables, bed trials, furniture, skins, and floors) and patient care equipment (eg: stethoscope, blood pressure cuffs *etc*).
    b) Exposure to this contaminated environment causes the MRSA infection.
    c) Cleaning and disinfection is a part of the practices to prevent transmission. Therefore, effective environmental cleaning practices is a valued objective in healthcare settings (134).
7. Educate Health Care Personnel (HCP) about MRSA
    a) The effective key component of the MRSA prevention program involves the modification of HCP behavior (eg, hand hygiene, environmental cleaning, and disinfection). They should be educated about their role in MRSA prevention (133,135).
8. Educate patients and their families about MRSA
    a) A proper education must be provided to the patients and their family about MRSA prevention which may help to reduce the risk of developing an asymptomatic infection, the risk of transmission to other members of the family, visitors *etc* (136).
9. Special approaches

Special approaches are mainly recommended to the hospitals with a higher rate of MRSA (29).

    a. Antibiotic stewardship:

Prevalence and Detection of Methicillin Resistant *Staphylococcus aureus* (MRSA)

The antibiotic should be given at a correct dosage and for an appropriate duration. Use of broad-spectrum antibiotics, particularly third-generation cephalosporins and fluoroquinolones should be reduced (131).

b. Screening:

Active screening of patients for MRSA carriage should be performed and the results should be linked to a targeted approach to the use of isolation and cohorting facilities. High-risk patients should be screened routinely. The fine detail regarding which patients are screened should be determined locally by the infection control team (134).

c. Antimicrobial testing

Antimicrobial testing should be performed to standardized accurate qualitative and quantitative results. This helps in controlling the infection caused by the microorganism at a higher rate (137).

10
CONCLUSION

Methicillin-resistant *Staphylococcus aureus* (MRSA) is a major nosocomial pathogen causing significant morbidity and mortality. The epidemiology of MRSA has continued to evolve since its first appearance more than three decades ago. Epidemic strains of these MRSA are usually resistant to several other antibiotics. During the past 15 years, the appearance and worldwide spread of many such clones have caused major therapeutic problems in many hospitals as well as the diversion of considerable resources to attempts at controlling their spread.

It has been seen that the increasing prevalence of MRSA infections in the hospitals, other care centers and in the community has become a worldwide phenomenon. The widespread of the multi-drug resistant strains and the antibiotic clones of the bacteria is worrying as it complicates the diagnosis and chemotherapies. There is a need for the adequate policy framework on infection control that will reflect the current epidemiologic characters of MRSA as well as the strict implementation of such control program to checkmate the spread of MRSA infections.

MRSA and now vancomycin resistance has also resulted in a steady decline in efficacy of these antibiotics. MRSA is no longer only an infection that is acquired in hospitals (HA-MRSA), although this remains a primary source of transmission. The incidence of HA and CA-MRSA infections as well as their prevalence varies considerably among countries. Some of the MRSA clones lineages are more frequently isolated than others owing to their survival and transmissibility. The HA-MRSA is endemic in many hospitals worldwide.

The MRSA has markedly influenced the empirical therapy for *Staphylococcal* infections. Limited therapeutic options are available for the management of these infections. Most β-lactam antibiotics are ineffective against both HA and CA-MRSA. The HA-MRSA is usually MDR. Resistance to β-lactam drugs varies geographically and may change over time. The infections were treated with oral antibiotics including doxycycline, minocycline, clindamycin, trimethoprim-sulfamethoxazole, rifampicin and fusidic acid. Severe HA-MRSA infections demand intravenous vancomycin therapy. Transmission can be prevented by following infection control strategies and

Prevalence and Detection of Methicillin Resistant *Staphylococcus aureus* (MRSA)

decolonization therapy. The key to MRSA control is the early treatment of MRSA infections and the following of good infection control practices. As only limited drugs are available for the treatment of MRSA, irrational use of antibiotics should be avoided and a rational antibiotic policy must be adopted.

11
FUTURE PERSPECTIVE

The challenges for the future are to minimize the infection while limiting the emergence of antibiotic-resistant organisms with optimal cost-effective care. There is an urgent need for clinical studies to evaluate strategies for the prevention and management of such infection in critically ill patients. There is a need for the education of healthcare workers on the importance of these bacteria and their modes of spreading. Emphasis must be laid on various infection control measures such as adequate hand washing techniques, aseptic measures for all procedures, antibiotic cycling and health education for the health personnel.

The clinical isolates should be processed for further biochemical identification (biotyping), analyzed possible by more than one molecular strain typing method, screened to obtain a complete profile of virulence and antibiotic resistance determinants (often using genotypic and phenotypic methods). However, only through these efforts, a complete understanding of the pathogenesis of clinical infection can be achieved. This will help in future strategies to aim at controlling the serious problems with a huge impact in terms of patient morbidity and social and economic costs.

12
REFERENCES

1) Rybak MJ, Pharm D, Laplante KL, Pharm D. *Staphylococcus aureus* : a review. Pharmacotherapy. 2005;25(1):74-85.

2) Rasmussen R V, Jr VGF, Skov R, Bruun NE.Future challenge and treatment of *Staphylococcus aureus*. Future Microbiology. 2011 Jan;6(1):43–56.

3) Chugh TD. Mini-review article *Staphylococcus aureus*. Journal of Infections in Developing Countries. 2007;1(2):125–8.

4) Joshi S, Ray P, Manchanda V, Bajaj J, Chitnis DS, Gautam V, *et. al.,* Methicillin resistant *Staphylococcus aureus* (MRSA) in India : prevalence & susceptibility pattern. Indian Journal of Medical Research. 2013 Feb;137(2):363–9.

5) D'Souza N, Rodrigues C, Mehta A. Molecular characterization of methicillin-resistant *Staphylococcus aureus* with emergence of epidemic clones of sequence type (ST) 22 and ST 772 in Mumbai,India. Journal of Clinical Microbiology. 2010;48(5):1806–11.

6) Boutiba-Ben Boubaker, R. Ben Abbes, Ben Abdallah, K. Mamlouk, F. Mahjoubi, Kammoun AH, SBR. Evaluation of a cefoxitin disk diffusion test for the routine detection of methicillin- resistant *Staphylococcus aureus*. Clinical Microbiology of Infections. 2004;10(8):762–5.

7) Baillargeon J, Kelley MJ, Leach CT, Baillargeon G, Pollock BH. Methicillin-resistant *Staphylococcus aureus* infection in the texas prison system. Clinical Infectious Diseases. 2004;38:392-395.

8) Methicillin-resistant *Staphylococcus aureus* (MRSA) Guidance for nursing staff MRSA – key facts.

9) Grem HA, Geidam YA, Gadzama GB, Ameh JA, Suleiman A. Methicillin resistant *Staphylococcus aureus* (MRSA) :review article. Advances in Animal and Veterinary Science. 2015;3(2):79-98.

10) Katayama Y, Ito T, Hiramatsu K. Genetic organization of the chromosome region surrounding mecA in clinical Staphylococcal strains : Role of IS 431 - mediated mecI deletion in expression of resistance resistant Staphylococcus haemolyticus. Antimicrobial Agents and Chemotherapy. 2001;45(7):1955–63.

11) Stapleton PD, Taylor PW. Methicillin resistance in *Staphylococcus aureus*: mechanism and modulation. Science Progress. 2007;85(Pt 1):1–14.

12) Sakoulas G, Gold HS, Venkataraman L, Degirolami PC, Eliopoulos GM, Qian Q. Methicillin-resistant *Staphylococcus aureus*: comparison of susceptibility testing methods and analysis of mecA -positive susceptible strains. Journal of Clinical Microbiology. 2001 Nov;39(11):3946–51.

13) Autiero I, Costantini S, Colonna G. Modeling of the bacteria mechanism of methicillin-resistance by a systems biology approach. PLoS One. 2009;4(7).

14) Appelbaum PC. MRSA — the tip of the iceberg. Clinical Microbiology and Infection. 2006 Apr;12(2):3-10.

15) Borg MA, Kraker M De, Scicluna E, Sande-bruinsma N Van De, Tiemersa E, Monen J, et.al. Prevalence of methicillin-resistant *Staphylococcus aureus* (MRSA) in invasive isolates from southern and eastern Mediterranean countries. Journal of Antimicrobial Chemotherapy. 2007 Dec;60(6):1310–5.

16) Buzaid N, Elzouki A, Taher I, Ghenghesh KS. Methicillin-resistant *Staphylococcus aureus* (MRSA) in a tertiary surgical and trauma hospital in Benghazi, Libya. Journal of Infections in Developing Countries. 2011 Oct 13;5(10):723–6.

17) Tiwari HK, Das AK, Sapkota D, Sivarajan K, Kumar V. Methicillin resistant *Staphylococcus aureus*: prevalence and antibiogram in a tertiary care hospital in western Nepal. Journal of Infection in Developinf Countries. 2009 Oct 22;3(9):681-4.

18) Tyagi A, Kapil A, Singh P. Incidence of Methicillin Resistant Stahylococcus aureus (MRSA) in Pus Samples at a tertiary care hospital, AIIMS, New Delhi. Journal of Indian Association of Clinical Medicine. 2008;9(1):33–5.

19) Tsering DC, Pal R, Kar S. Methicillin-resistant *Staphylococcus aureus*: prevalence and current susceptibility pattern in Sikkim. Journal of Global Infectious Disease. 2011 Jan;3(1):9-13.

20) Saxena S, Singh K, Talwar V. Methicillin-resistant *Staphylococcus aureus* prevalence in community in the East Delhi Area. Japanese Journal of Infectious Disease. 2003 Apr;56(2):54–6.

21) Davis KA, Stewart JJ, Crouch HK, Florez CE, Hospenthal DR. Methicillin-resistant *Staphylococcus aureus* (MRSA) nares colonization at hospital admission and its effect on subsequent MRSA Infection. Clinical Infectious Disease. 2004 Sep 15;39(6):776-82.

22) Pramodhini S, Thenmozhivalli PR, Selvi R, Dillirani V, Vasumathi A, Agatha D. Comparison of various phenotypic methods and mecA based PCR for the detection of MRSA. Journal of Clinical and Diagnostic Research. 2011;20(7):1359–62.

23) Patil NR, Ghorpade M V. Comparison of conventional phenotypic methods for detection of methicillin resistant *Staphylococcus aureus*. International Journal of Research and Development in Pharmacy and Life Sciences. 2016;5(2):2039–44.

24) Priya NL, Venkatesh KG, Sumathi G, Geethalakshmi S. Detection of Methicillin Resistant Strains of *Staphylococcus aureus* using phenotypic and genotypic methods in a tertiary care hospital. International Journal of Current Microbiology and Applied Science. 2017;6(7):4008–14.

25) Panda RK, Mahapatra A, Mallick B, Chayani N. Evaluation of genotypic and phenotypic methods for detection of methicillin resistant *Staphylococcus aureus* in a tertiary care hospital of Eastern Odisha. Journal of Clinical and Diagnostic Research. 2016 Feb;10(2):19–21.

26) Krishnan PU, Miles K, Shetty N. Detection of methicillin and mupirocin resistance in *Staphylococcus aureus* isolates using conventional and molecular methods: a descriptive study from a burns unit with high prevalence of MRSA. Journal of Clinical Pathology. 2002 Oct;55(10):745-748.

27) Enright MC, Day NPJ, Davies CE, Peacock SJ. Multilocus sequence typing for characterization of methicillin-resistant and methicillin-susceptible clones of *Staphylococcus aureus*. Journal of Clinical Microbiology. 2000 Mar;38(3):1008–15.

28) Huletsky A, Giroux R, Rossbach V, Gagnon M, Vaillancourt M, Bernier M, *et. al.,* New real-time PCR assay for rapid detection of methicillin-resistant *Staphylococcus aureus* directly from specimens containing a mixture of Staphylococci. Journal of Clinical Micobiology. 2004 May;42(5):1875–84.

29) Calfee DP, Salgado CD, Milstone AM, Harriss AD, Kuhar Dt, Moody J, et.al. Strategies to prevent methicillin-resistant *Staphylococcus aureus* transmission and infection in acute care hospitals : 2014 Update. Infection Control and Hospital Epidemiology. 2014 Jul;3(7):772–96.

30) Topley and Wilson's. Microbiology and microbial infections, 2 Volume Set: Bacteriology,10th edition. S. Peter Borriello, Patrick R. Murray GF, editor. 771-831 p.

31) Burden of Resistance to Methicillin- Resistant *Staphylococcus aureus*. A fact sheet from ReAct- action on antibiotic resistance. 2008 May.

32) Elmer W. Koneman, Gary W. Procop MD, MS. Textbook of Diagnostic Microbiology. 5th edition. 2016. 623-671 p.

33) Thomas WD, Archer GL. Mobility of gentamicin resistance genes from staphylococci isolated in the United States: identification of Tn4031, a gentamicin resistance transposon from Staphylococcus epidermidis. Antimicrobial Agents and Chemotherapy. 1989;33(8):1335–41.

34) Roth RR, James WD. Microbiology of the skin : resident flora, ecology, infection. Journal of the American Academy of Dematology. 1989 Mar;20(3):367-3

35) Mandell, Douglas B. Principles and Practice of infectious disease. 6th edition. John E. Bennett MD MACP, Raphael Dolin M, editor. Vol.I 192:2321-2351.

36) Weinstein, R.A., S.A. Kabins . Gentamicin-resistant Staphylococci as hospital flora : epidemiology and resistance plasmids. Antimicrobial Agents and Chemotherapy. 1982;21(3):145:374-382.

37) Vidhani S, Mehndiratta PL, MM. Study of methicillin resistant S. aureus (MRSA) isolates from high risk patients. Indian Journal of Medical Microbiology. 2001;19(2):13–6.

38) Williams RE. L forms of *Staphylococcus aureus*. Journal of General Microbiology. 1963;33:325-334.

39) Kenneth JR, Ray CG. Spread and Control of Infection. Sherris Medical Microbiology. 2004. 173-258 p.

40) Mackie and McCartney. Baird.D:Staphylococcus: cluster-forming gram-positive cocci. Mackie & McCartney: practical medical microbiology. 14th edition. J.G.Collee, A.G.Fraser, B.P..Marmion AS, editor. Elsevier; 1996. 245-261 p.

41) Dan M, Marien GJ, Goldsand G. Endocarditis caused by Staphylococcus warneri on a normal aortic valve following vasectomy. Canadian Medical Association Journal. 1984 Aug 1;131(3):211–3.

42) Hollyoak V. Guidelines on the control of methicillin-resistant *Staphylococcus aureus* in the community. Journal of Hospital Infections. 1996;32(1):81–2.

43) Freer JH, Arbuthnoti JP. Toxins of *Staphylococcus aureus*. Pharmacology and Therapeutics. 1982;19(1):55–106.

44) Otto M. *Staphylococcus aureus* toxins. Current Opinion in Microbiology. 2014;17(1):32–7.

45) Ladhani S, Joannou CL, Lochrie DP, Evans RW, Poston SM. Clinical, microbial, and biochemical aspects of the exfoliative toxins causing staphylococcal scalded-skin syndrome. Clinical Microbiology Reviews. 1999;12(2):224–42.

46) Tinetti ME, Baker DG. Acute monoarthritis. New England Journal of Medicine. 1988 Sep 30;329(14):1013-20.

47) Fowler VG, Olsen MK, Corey GR, Cheng AC, Dudley T, Oddone EZ, et.al. Clinical identifiers of complicated S. aureus bacteremia. Archieves of Internal Medicine. 2003 Sep 22;163(17):2066–72.

48) Gillet Y, Issartel B, Vanhems P, Fournet JC, Lina G, Bes M, *et. al.,* Association between *Staphylococcus aureus* strains carrying gene for panton-valentine leukocidin and highly lethal necrotising pneumonia in young immunocompetent patients. Lancet. 2002;359(9308):753–9.

49) Tomasz R. A. M. Beta-Lactam antibiotic resistance in gram-positive bacterial pathogens of the upper respiratory tract: a brief overview of mechanisms. Microbiological Drug Resistance. 1995;1(2):103–9.

50) Batabyal B, Kundu GKR, Biswas S. Methicillin-resistant *Staphylococcus aureus* : a brief review. International Research Journal of Biological Sciences. 2012 Nov;1(7):65–71.

51) Chambers HF. Methicillin-resistant staphylococci. Clinical Microbiology Reviews. 1988 Apr;1(2):173–86.

52) Tang YT, Cao R, Xiao N, Li ZS, Wang R, Zou JM, *et. al.,* Molecular epidemiology and antimicrobial susceptibility of methicillin-resistant *Staphylococcus aureus* isolates in Xiangyang, China. Journal of Global Antimicrobial Resistance. 2018;12:31–6.

53) Methicillin Resistant *Staphylococcus aureus.* The Center for Food Security and Public Health. 2016 May;1–27.

54) Skov R, Faria NA, Oleiveira DC, Westh H, Monnet DL, Larsen AR, et.al. Epidemiology of emerging methicillin-resistant *Staphylococcus aureus* in Denmark. Journal of Clinical Microbiology. 2005 Apr;43(4):1836–42.

55) Guzmán-blanco M, Mejía C, Isturiz R, Alvarez C, Bavestrello L, Gotuzzo E, *et. al.,* Epidemiology of methicillin-resistant *Staphylococcus aureus* (MRSA) in Latin America. International Journal of Antimicrobial Agents. 2009;34:304–8.

56) Ray P, Gautam V, Singh R. Methicillin-resistant *Staphylococcus aureus* (MRSA) in developing and developed countries : implications and solutions. Indian Journal of Critical Care Medicine. 2011;15(1):74–82.

57) Hiramatsu K, Kayayama Y, Matsuo M, Aiba Y, Saito M, Hishinuma T, *et. al.,* Vancomycin-intermediate resistance in *Staphylococcus aureus.* Journal of Global Antimicrobial Resistance. 2014;2(4):213–24.

58) Hiramatsu K, Aritaka N, Hanaki H, Kawasaki S, Hosoda Y, Hori S, *et. al.,* Dissemination in Japanese hospitals of strains of *Staphylococcus aureus* heterogeneously resistant to vancomycin. Lancet. 1997;350(9092):1670–3.

59) Gardete S, Tomasz A. Mechanisms of vancomycin resistance in *Staphylococcus aureus.* Journal of Clinical Investigation. 2014;124(7).

60) Gardete S, Tomasz A. Mechanisms of vancomycin resistance in *Staphylococcus aureus.* Journal of Clinical Investigation. 2014;124(7):2836–40.

61) Bishara J, Goldberg E, Leibovici L, Samra Z, Shaked H, Mansur N, *et. al.,* Healthcare-associated vs. hospital-acquired *Staphylococcus aureus* bacteremia. International Journal of Infectious Diseases. 2012;16(6):e457–63.

62) Fukunaga BT, Sumida WK, Taira DA, Davis JW, Seto TB. Hospital-acquired methicillin-resistant *Staphylococcus aureus* bacteremia related to medicare antibiotic prescriptions: a state-level analysis. Hawaii Journal of Medicine and Public Health. 2016;75(10):303–

63) Smith K, Gemmell CG, Hunter IS. The association between biocide tolerance and the presence or absence of qac genes among hospital-acquired and community-acquired MRSA isolates. Journal of Antimicrobial Chemotherapy. 2008;61(1):78–84.

64) Wernitz MH, Swidsinksi S, Weist K, Sohr D, White W, Franke KP, *et. al.,* Effectiveness of a hospital-wide selective screening programme for methicillin-resistant *Staphylococcus aureus* (MRSA) carriers at hospital admission to prevent hospital-acquired MRSA infections. Clinical Microbiology and Infections. 2005;11(6):457–65.

65) Herold BC, Immergluck LC, Maranan MC, Lauderdale DS, Gaskin RE, Boyle-vavra S, *et. al.,* Community-acquired methicillin-resistant *Staphylococcus aureus* in children with no identified predisposing risk. JAMA. 1998;279(8):593–8.

66) Vandenesch F, Naimi T, Enright MC, Lina G, Nimmo GR, Heffernan H, *et. al.,* Community-acquired methicillin-resistant *Staphylococcus aureus* carrying panton-valentine leukocidin genes: worldwide emergence. Emerging Infectious Diseases. 2003;9(8):978–84.

67) Salmenlinna S, Lyytikäinen O, Vuopio-Varkila J. Community-acquired methicillin-resistant *Staphylococcus aureus*, Finland. Emerging Infectious Diseases. 2002;8(6):602–7.

68) Huang H, Flynn NM, King JH, Monchaud C, Morita M, Cohen SH. Comparisons of community-associated methicillin-resistant *Staphylococcus aureus* (MRSA) and hospital-associated MSRA infections in Sacramento, California. Journal of Clinical Microbiology. 2006;44(7):2423–7.

69) Stapleton PD, Taylor PW. Methicillin resistance in *Staphylococcus aureus*: mechanisms and modulation. Science Progress. 2007;85(Pt 1):1–14.

70) Lowy FD. Antimicrobial resistance: the example of *Staphylococcus aureus*. Journal of Clinical Investigation. 2003;111(9):1265–73.

71) Berger-Bachi B. Genetic basis of methicillin resistance in *Staphylococcus aureus*. Cellular and Molecular Life Sciences. 1999 Nov 30;56(9–10):764–70.

72) Jensen S, Lyon B. Genetics of antimicrobial resistance in *Staphylococcus aureus*. Future Microbiology. 2009 Jun;4(5):565–582.

73) Katayama Y, Ito T, Hiramatsu K. A new class of genetic element, staphylococcus cassette chromosome mec, encodes methicillin resistance in *Staphylococcus aureus*. Journal of Antimicrobial Agents and Chemotherapy. 2000;44(6):1549–55.

74) Ito T, Katayama Y, Asada K, Mori N, Tsutsumimoto K. Structural Comparison of three types of staphylococcal cassette chromosome mec integrated in the chromosome in methicillin-resistant *Staphylococcus aureus*. Journal of Antimicrobial Agents and Chemotherapy. 2001;45(5):1323–36.

75) Couto I, Wu SW, Tomasz A, Lencastre H De. Development of methicillin resistance in clinical isolates of Staphylococcus sciuri by transcriptional activation of the mecA homologue native to the species development of methicillin resistance in clinical isolates of Staphylococcus sciuri by transcript. Journal of Bacteriology. 2003;185(2):645–53.

76) Jayaweera AS, Karunarathnane M, Kumbukgolla WW, Thushari HL. Prevalence of methicillin resistant *Staphylococcus aureus* (MRSA) bacteremia at Teaching Hospital Anuradhapura , Sri Lanka. Ceylon Medical Journal. 2017 Mar;62:110–1.

77) Suryadevara VD, Basavaraju A, Vasireddy K. Prevalence of MRSA among clinical isolates and their antibiogram in a tertiary care hospital. Journal of Evolution of Medical and Dental Science. 2017 Mar 13;6(21):1667–9.

78) Pandya N, Chaudhary A, Mehta S, Parmar R. Characterization of methicillin resistant *Staphylococcus aureus* from various clinical samples at tertiary care hospital of rural Gujarat. International Journal of Health Science and Research. 2015;5(9):202-206.

79) Saikia L, Nath R, Choudhury B, Sarkar M. Prevalence and antimicrobial susceptibility pattern of methicillin-resistant *Staphylococcus aureus* in assam. Indian Journal of Critical Care and Medicine. 2009;13(3):156–158.

80) Pai V, Rao V, Rao SP. Prevalence and antimicrobial susceptibility pattern of methicillin-resistant *Staphylococcus aureus* (MRSA) isolates at a tertiary care hospital in Mangalore,South India. Journal of Laboratory Physicians. 2010 Jul-Dec;2(2):82-84.

81) Khadri H, Alzohairy M. Prevalence and antibiotic susceptibility pattern of methicillin-resistant and coagulase-negative staphylococci in a tertiary care hospital in India. International Journal of Medicine and Medical Science. 2010Apr;2(4):116–20.

82) Ranjan KP, Ranjan N, Gandhi S. Surgical site infections with special reference to methicillin resistant *Staphylococcus aureus* : experience from a tertiary care referral hospital in North India. International Journal of Research in Medical Science. 2013 May;1(2):108–11.

83) Frazee BW, Lynn J, Lambert L, Lowery D. High prevalence of methicillin-resistant *Staphylococcus aureus* in emergency department skin and soft tissue infections. Annals of Emergency Medicine. 2005 Mar;45(3):311–20.

84) Joachim A, Moyo SJ, Nkinda L, Majigo M, Mmbaga E, Mbembati N. Prevalence of methicillin-resistant *Staphylococcus aureus* carriage on admission among patients attending regional hospitals in Dar es Salaam,Tanzania. BMC Research Notes. 2017 Aug 22;10(1):417.

Prevalence and Detection of Methicillin Resistant *Staphylococcus aureus* (MRSA)

85) Pourmand MR, Hassanzadeh S, Mashhadi R, Askari E. Comparison of four diagnostic methods for detection of methicillin resistant *Staphylococcus aureus*. Iranian Journal of Microbiology. 2014;6(5):341–4.

86) CLSI. Performance standards for antimicrobial susceptibility testing. 27th edition. 2017. 282 p.

87) Anand K. B, Agrawal P, Kumar S, Kapila K. Comparison of cefoxitin disc diffusion test, oxacillin screen agar, and PCR for mecA gene for detection of MRSA. Indian Journal of Medical Microbiology. 2009 Jan-Mar;27(1):27-9.

88) Antunes ALS, Secchi C, Reiter KC, Perez LRR, De Freitas ALP, D'Azevedo PA. Evaluation of oxacillin and cefoxitin disks for detection of resistance in coagulase negative staphylococci. International Journal of Biological and Biomedical research. 2007;102(6):719–23.

89) Rabelo MA, Monteiro A, Neto B, Luis W, Oliveira M De, Lopes ACS, *et. al.,* Phenotypic methods for determination of methicillin resistance in *Staphylococcus* spp . from health care workers. Brazilian Journal of Pathology and Laboratory Medicine. 2013 Apr;49(2):91–6.

90) Clinical and Laboratory Standards Institute (CLSI). Preventing pneumococcal disease among infants and young children. Recommendations of the Advisory Committee on Immunization Practices (ACIP). Vol. 33, 2011. 1-35 p.

91) Fatani AJ Baddour MM, Abueikheir MM. Comparison of mecA polymerase chain reaction with phenotypic methods for the detection of methicillin-resistant *Staphylococcus aureus*. Current Microbiology. 2007 Dec;55(6):473–9.

92) Wayne P. Performance Standarts for Antimicrobial Disk Susceptibility Tests; Approved Standard; 9 Edition. Vol. 26, Clinical and laboratory standards institute. 2006.

93) Skov R, Smyth R, Larsen AR, Bolmstro A, Karlsson A, Mills K, *et. al.,* Phenotypic detection of methicillin resistance in *Staphylococcus aureus* by disk diffusion testing and Etest on mueller-hinton agar. Journal of Clinical Microbiology. 2006;44(12):4395–9.

94) Luber P, Bartelt E, Genschow E, Wagner J, Hahn H. Comparison of broth microdilution , E test , and agar dilution methods for antibiotic susceptibility testing of Campylobacter jejuni and Campylobacter coli. Journal of Clinical Microbiology. 2003;41(3):1062–8.

95) To WK, Fothergill AW, Rinaldi MG. Comparative evaluation of macrodilution and alamar colorimetric microdilution broth methods for antifungal susceptibility testing of yeast isolates. Journal of Clinical Microbiology. 1995;33(10):2660–4.

96) Weinstein, M. P. Methods for dilution antimicrobial susceptibility tests for bacteria that grow aerobically ; approved standard — Ninth Edition. 2012 Vol. 32(2). 18 p.

97) Colombo AL, Barchiesi F, Gough D a MC. Comparison of E test and national committee for clinical laboratory standards broth macrodilution method for azole antifungal susceptibility testing . Journal of Clinical Microbiology. 1995;33(3):535–40.

98) Lim D, Strynadka NC. Structural basis for the β lactam resistance of PBP2a from methicillin-resistant *Staphylococcus aureus*. Nature Structural Biology. 2002 Nov;9(11):870-6.

99) Hal SJ Van, Stark D, Lockwood B, Marriott D, Harkness J. Methicillin-resistant *Staphylococcus aureus* (MRSA) detection : comparison of two molecular methods (IDI-MRSA PCR assay and genotype MRSA direct PCR assay) with three selective MRSA agars (MRSA ID , MRSA Select , and CHROMagar MRSA) for use with infection control swabs. Journal of Clinical Microbilogy. 2007 Aug;45(8):2486–90.

100) Ercis S, Sancak B, Hascelik G. Comparison of PCR detection of mecA with oxacillin disk susceptibility testing in different media and sceptor automated system for both *Staphylococcus aureus* and coagulase negative Staphylococcus isolates. Indian Journal of Medical Microbiology. 2008;26(1):21-4.

101) Lencastre HDE, Figueiredo AMSA, Urban C, Rahal J, Tomasz A. Multiple mechanisms of methicillin resistance and improved methods for detection in clinical isolates of *Staphylococcus aureus*. Antimicrobial Agents and Chemotherapy. 1991 Apr;35(4):632–9.

102) Datta P, Gulati N, Singla N, Vasdeva HR, Bala K. Evaluation of various methods for the detection of meticillin-resistant *Staphylococcus aureus* strains and susceptibility patterns. Journal of Medical Microbiology. 2011;(60):1613–6.

103) Aghamali M, Rahbar M, Samadi H. Laboratory methods for identification of methicillin-resistant *Staphylococcus aureus*. Reviews in Medical Microbiology. 2017 Aug 3; 27.

104) Chapin KC, Musgnug MC. Evaluation of penicillin binding protein 2a latex agglutination assay for identification of methicillin-resistant *Staphylococcus aureus* directly from blood cultures. Journal of Clinical Microbiology. 2004;42(3):1283–5.

105) Van Griethuysen A, Pouw M, van Leeuwen N, Heck M, Willemse P, Buiting A, *et. al.,* Rapid slide latex agglutination test for detection of methicillin resistance in *Staphylococcus aureus*. Journal of Clinical Microbiology. 1999 Sep;37(9):2789–92.

106) Knapp CC, Ludwig MD, Washington JA. Evaluation of BBL crystals MRSA ID system. Journal of Clinical Microbiology. 1994;32(10):2588–9.

107) Brown DFJ, Edwards DI, Hawkey PM, Morrison D, Ridgway GL, Towner KJ, *et. al.,* Guidelines for the laboratory diagnosis and susceptibility testing of methicillin-resistant *Staphylococcus aureus* (MRSA). Journals of Antimicrobial Chemotherapy. 2005;56(6):1000–18.

108)Bignardi GE, Woodford N, Chapman A, Johnson AP, Speller DCE. Detection of the mec-A gene and pbenotypic detection of resistance in *Staphylococcus aureus* isolates with borderline or low-level methicillin resistance. Journal of Antimicrobial Chemotherapy. 1996;37:53–63.

109)Lencastre H De, De souza MA. Evolution of sporadic isolates of methicillin-resistant *Staphylococcus aureus* (MRSA) in hospitals and their similarities to isolates of community-acquired MRSA. Journal of Clinical Microbiology. 2003;41(8):3806–15.

110)Krishnan PU, Miles K, Shetty N. Detection of methicillin and mupirocin resistance in *Staphylococcus aureus* isolates using conventional and molecular methods: a descriptive study from a burns unit with high prevalencec of MRSA. Journal of Clinical Pathology. 2002;55(1):745–8.

111)Mathur P, Bhardwaj N, Gupta G, Dahiya R, Behera B, Misra M, *et. al.,* Resistance pattern of mupirocin in methicillin-resistant *Staphylococcus aureus* in trauma patients and comparison between disc diffusion and E-test for better detection of resistance in low resource countries. Journal of Laboratory Physicians. 2014;6(2):91.

112)Malaviolle X, Nonhoff C, Denis O, Rottiers S, Struelens MJ. Evaluation of disc diffusion methods and Vitek 2 automated system for testing susceptibility to mupirocin in *Staphylococcus aureus*. Journal of Antimicrobial Chemotherapy. 2008;62(5):1018–23.

113)Krishnan PU, Miles K, Shetty N. Detection of methicillin and mupirocinresistance in *Staphylococcus aureus* isolates using conventional and molecular methods. Journal of Clinical Pathology. 2002;55:745-748.

114)Maiden MCJ, Bygraves JA, Feil E, Morelli G, Russell JE, Urwin R, *et. al.,* Multilocus sequence typing: A portable approach to the identification of clones within populations of pathogenic microorganisms. Proceeding of the National Academy of Sciences of the United States of America. 1998;95(6):3140–5.

115)Spratt B. Multilocus sequence typing: molecular typing of bacterial pathogens in an era of rapid {DNA} sequencing and the internet. Current Opinion in Microbiology. 1999;2(3):312–6.

116)Solyman SM, Black CC, Duim B, Perreten V, Van Duijkeren E, Wagenaar JA, *et. al.,* Multilocus sequence typing for characterization of Staphylococcus pseudintermedius. Journal of Clinical Microbiology. 2013;51(1):306–10.

117)Berglund C, Molling P, Sjoberg L, Soderquist B. Multilocus sequence typing of methicillin-resistant *Staphylococcus aureus* from an area of low endemicity by real-time PCR. Journal of Clinical Microbiology. 2005;43(9):4448–54.

Prevalence and Detection of Methicillin Resistant *Staphylococcus aureus* (MRSA)

118)Enright MC, Robinson DA, Randle G, Feil EJ, Grundmann H, Spratt BG. The evolutionary history of methicillin-resistant *Staphylococcus aureus* (MRSA). Proceeding of the National Academy of Sciences of the United States of America 2002 May28;99(11):7687-92.

119)Savor C, Pfaller MA, Kruszynski JA, Hollis RJ, Noskin GA, Peterson LR. Comparison of genomic methods for differentiating strains of Euterococcus faecium : assessment using clinical epidemiologic data. Journal of Clinical Microbiology. 1998;36(11):3327–31.

120)Strandén A, Frei R, Widmer AF. Molecular typing of methicillin-resistant *Staphylococcus aureus*: can PCR replace pulsed-field gel electrophoresis. Journal of Clinical Microbiology. 2003;41(7):3181–6.

121)Tenover FC, Arbeit RD, Goering R V., Mickelsen PA, Murray BE, Persing DH, *et. al.,* Interpreting chromosomal DNA restriction patterns produced by pulsed-field gel electrophoresis: criteria for bacterial strain typing. Journal of Clinical Microbiology. 1995;33(9):2233–9.

122)Petersdorf S, Oberdorfer K, Wendt C. Longitudinal study of the molecular epidemiology of methicillin-resistant *Staphylococcus aureus* at a University Hospital. Journal of Clinical Microbiology. 2006;44(12):4297–302.

123)Ke D, Picard FJ, Martineau F, Menard C, Roy PH, Ouellette M, *et. al.,* Development of a PCR assay for rapid detection of enterococci. Journal of Clinical Microbiology. 1999;37(11):3497–503.

124)Martineau F, Picard FJ, Ménard C, Roy PH, Ouellette M, Bergeron MG. Development of a rapid PCR assay specific for Staphylococcus saprophyticus and application to direct detection from urine samples. Journal of Clinical Microbiology. 2000;38(9):3280–4.

125)Adkins S, Burmeister M. Visualization of DNA in agarose gels as migrating colored bands: applications for preparative gels and educational demonstrations. Analytical Biochemistry. 1996;240(1):17–23.

126)Martineau F, Picard FJ, Ke D, Paradis S, Roy PH, Ouellete M, *et. al.,* Development of a PCR assay for identification of Staphylococci at genus and species levels. Journal of Clinical Microbiology. 2001;39(7):2541–7.

127)Sambrook J, Green MR. Molecular cloning, A laboratory Manual. Vol. 33, Zoological Research. 2012. 75-78 p.

128)Grubb WB, Brien FGO, Coombs GW, Pearson JC, Christiansen KJ. Type V Staphylococcal cassette chromosome mec in community staphylococci from australia. Antimicrobial Agents of Chemotherapy. 2005;49(12):5129–32.

129)Woodside J. Guide to infection prevention in emergency medical services. APIC Implementation Guide. 2013.

Prevalence and Detection of Methicillin Resistant *Staphylococcus aureus* (MRSA)

130)Siegel J, Strausbaugh L, Jackson M, Rhinehart E, Chiarello L a. The draft guideline for isolation precautions: preventing transmission of infectious agents in healthcare settings 2007.

131)Coia JE, Duckworth GJ, Edwards DI, Farrington M, Fry C, Humphreys H, *et. al.,* Guidelines for the control and prevention of meticillin-resistant *Staphylococcus aureus* (MRSA) in healthcare facilities. Journal of Hospital Infection. 2006;63:S1–44.

132)Siegel JD, Rhinehart E, Jackson M, Chiarello L. 2007 Guideline for isolation precautions: preventing transmission of infectious agents in health care settings.

133)Gopal Rao G, Jeanes A, Osman M, Aylott C, Green J. Marketing hand hygiene in hospitals: a case study. Journal of Hospital Infections. 2002;50(1):42–7.

134)Aureden K, Arias K, Burns LA, Creen C, Hickok J, Moody J, *et. al.,* Guide to the elimination of *Staphylococcus aureus* (MRSA) transmission in hospital settings. 2010. 1-65 p.

135)Stelfox HT, Bates DW, Redelmeier DA. Safety of patients isolated for infection control. JAMA. 2003;290(14):1899–905.

136)Prevention of MRSA Infections in Hospitals. 2012 Jan.

137)Damani N. Information resources in infection control. International Federation of Infection Control. 2004. 1-40 p.